Ten Influencing Skills

Ten Influencing Skills

Jan Bijker

Thema, publisher of Schouten Global, Zaltbommel, Th

Original title: *Tien beïnvloedingsvaardigheden*, Thema, Publisher of Schouten Global, Zaltbommel, The Netherlands

Production, English edition: Textcase, Utrecht, The Netherlands
Translation for Textcase: Rini Roerig, Hilversum, The Netherlands
nglish-language editor: Kate Santon, Gwynedd, Wales, United Kingdom
er design: Studio Jan de Boer, Amsterdam, The Netherlands
: Tekst2000, Houten, The Netherlands

0 5871 477 0

Contents

Foreword

The phenomenon of 'influence' has inspired many writers and thinkers to try and describe it, define it in theoretical models and find different perspectives on it. What struck me – in behavioural training and especially in discussions afterwards – is that most people are looking for the concrete behaviour that actually helps them to increase their influencing power. This sounds easier than it is. What is essential is that you are consciously willing to make an effort to find ways that, on the one hand, serve your own goals but which, at the same time, show respect for others stemming from your own convictions about integrity in communication. Attitude and being goal-oriented go hand in hand when applying effective behavioural skills. It is important that these behavioural skills are not just superficial tricks but that they become part and parcel of your own personality. Before you choose your behavioural style, it is necessary to be aware of what you want to achieve and how you want to achieve it. Also, you have to be able to assess the situation to know which type of behaviour is most likely to be successful.

These aspects will be dealt with in this book, but the emphasis here lies on using influencing skills in concrete behaviour. The work environment is our focus but it goes without saying that you can use your influencing skills in your private life as well. Personally, it has become increasingly difficult for me to separate my professional and my private life; when it comes to influencing skills, I operate in the same way in both worlds. Maybe I am more aware of how I apply influencing skills at work whereas there is more room for spontaneity in my private life. I learn a lot from people around me who give me feedback on how I influence them; it makes me more sensitive towards the person I am dealing with. Some friends think I am dominant and I try to take this into account; others say that I could be stricter and take a firmer position. In other words, influencing is a complex process between me and other people. Fine-tuning the process of being an excellent influencer will probably take the rest of my life. My hope is that you will be as fascinated by this phenomenon as I am.

I dedicate this book to some of the most influential people in my life: my partner Rini Roerig, who also translated this book. She was inspired by students from the Shri Ram College and the Miranda House in Delhi, India. My children Lenny and Dave and my faithful friends Jan de Buck, Frans Blom and Piet Vonk. My gratitude also goes to colleagues who have been critical and inspiring: Rob Bos, Bert van Dijk and Wim Geerts. Also thanks to Kenton Hall and John McCourt from Leicester, UK. You challenged us to give the training Influencing Skills in English. Thank you, Anneleen Siebelink and Berty Schaap for your excellent editing. Last but not least: readers and participants in the training sessions on Influencing Skills, thank you for your valuable feedback.

As is true for communication in general, you cannot *not* influence. The simple fact that you are somewhere, with other people, has an impact. Knowing this, my advice is to try to influence this impact as effectively as possible.

Jan Bijker
Hilversum, January 2008

1
An introduction

> About respect: *R-E-S-P-E-C-T: I know what it means to me.*
>
> Aretha Franklin
>
> And trust: *I know it's gonna work out fine.*
>
> Ike and Tina Turner

In Holland, the political and economic decision-making process is popularly referred to as the 'polder model', a model in which politics on the one hand and economic partners such as workers' and consumers' organisations on the other try to come to a consensus.

Every system has its pros and cons, but in the late 1990s objections to the effects of the polder model (endless negotiations and time-consuming decision-making procedures) were raised more frequently. Polarisation seemed more and more attractive: it creates clarity in different points of view and in profiling. The disadvantage, however, is that sometimes the debate becomes extreme and harsh. Now, at the beginning of the twenty-first century, we realize again that carefulness/mindfulness in debate and dialogue might be valuable. To take extreme positions and use force either appear not to work, or work only in the short term when you actually want to manage long-term changes.

The art of conducting effective meetings and creating the support which is sometimes necessary requires communication skills that influence people. Influencing from a position of distrust towards the other party does not work. The effect of trusting the other party is that you will get trust in return. Deserving trust can only be based on being able to give it yourself. Besides, trust in the other person and trust in the possibility of a solution create hope. And hope is what we need.

Despite the different cultural connotations of the word 'respect', many people from different cultures see it as an important value. Give and take seems to be an important aspect of showing respect. The influence of showing respect and giving trust should not be underestimated. Often this basic attitude invites the other person to do the same.

Food for thought: do you remember a situation in your own life where by showing your respect and giving your trust you made another person perform better or achieve more than was expected?

Getting results by giving respect and trust

Managers and consultants want results and need people to achieve these. The formal power that the manager has, but the consultant does not, is usually not enough to reach your goals. In Western Europe employees are now well-educated and reasonably assertive. They want meaningful work, pleasant circumstances and a certain degree of autonomy to realize the (company) goals. As a manager, you do not want to force your will upon an employee because you are bound to meet with resistance and cannot, therefore, be effective. A far more effective approach is to inspire employees so that they feel challenged, or to create circumstances that will keep them on board through their inner commitment and pride in the company. In order to do this, you need influencing skills.

This book is about the influencing skills you need in order to be effective in reaching your goals and achieving the company's results. Sometimes you hear negative reactions to influencing such as 'You manipulate people to get things your own way. That's not for me', but manipulation and influencing are two very different concepts. I am convinced that manipulation, as opposed to influencing, is risky. Manipulation, often coinciding with a hidden agenda, gives other people the uneasy feeling that they are being used and that there is no place whatsoever for their interests. There's no doubt that this will have a negative effect on the working relationship. Respectful conduct implies that you want to influence the other person without manipulation. Respect is an attitude; you deal with other people in the way in which you would want to be dealt with: do as you would be done by. Respecting the other person will result in the other person respecting you. And your influencing has already begun.

Trusting the other person works along the same lines. If you trust other people, you send a signal that they are being taken seriously – and this will result in them taking more responsibility for the contributions they are asked to give. By respect and trust, you also allow the other person to have influence. By realizing that there is room for mutual influencing, you have already been effective in your own influencing.

A far-reaching effect is that people will sometimes identify themselves to such an extent that they present ideas as if they were their own, when in fact you influenced them to embrace ideas that were originally yours. Ego, then, is of less importance to you as a manager if your employees commit to your ideas and goals and make them their own.

What will you find in this book?

In Chapter 2, I will give you two examples of effective influencing and the aspects that play a role when you influence other people.

In Chapter 3, I will pay attention to the strategic choices you have to make before you can choose the appropriate influencing skill. There is also a self-analysis questionnaire in this chapter that shows which influencing skills you already use, and to what extent. The ten influencing skills from which you can choose, based on your strategic choice, are described in Chapter 4. Also, switching gears in using the ten influencing styles will be discussed. Chapter 5 describes a case study illustrating that successful implementation requires this ability to change gears.

In Chapter 6, the issue of the middle manager's loyalty will get attention. Only when you can influence both your own manager as well as your team members can you solve that problem. Chapter 7 is devoted to consultants and the way they use their toolkit of ten influencing skills.

Another aspect of influencing but an equally important one is how to influence yourself. What hinders you in using a specific influencing skill? How can you deal with the irrationalities in your own mind? This is addressed in Chapter 8, in which the method of Rational Emotive Training is discussed, as well as how to influence others positively when they feel resistance.

2
What is influencing?

The answer, my friend, is blowing in the wind…

Bob Dylan

First consider this: influencing is not exerting power from a position of self-interest while being blind to the interests of others. Neither has it any bearing on having a hidden agenda, i.e. manipulation. Although manipulation might be successful if you think in the short term, the effect in the long run is that people will start to avoid you. Feeling used creates distrust and withdrawal.

The definition of 'influencing'

Influencing is a social process of interaction in which you want to reach your goals without formal power, with the consequence that people change their opinions or behaviour.

In this book, I especially focus on the skills and behaviour (interaction) that lead to effective influencing. There are more aspects, however, that play a role when influencing. I will illustrate this with the following example.

The influential manager
This man, Richard, has a special combination of characteristics. Sincere personal interest in and commitment to his employees go hand in hand with a clear focus on (company) goals. This becomes apparent during a conversation with a member of his management team: first, he shows true empathy and inquires after the personal development of his team member, but in the same conversation he also confronts the employee with the fact that he has failed to reach his targets. Theoretically, this could be confusing, but Richard's authenticity makes it acceptable. The goal of the feedback

he gives is to avoid such failure in the future without offending the team member concerned. In other words, Richard is tolerant towards the maker of the mistake, but not towards the mistake itself.

It is essential when influencing to:

- show sincere interest in the well-being of employees
- be clear in what you expect of others
- be clear in profiling yourself as managing director
- be goal oriented in combination with being challenging or creating commitment.

Here's another example.

The influential consultant
This woman, Jane, does not operate from an ivory tower, coming down to teach her client's company a lesson about how to improve their level of achievement. She sincerely investigated the problems her principal/client had and understood how he must feel in having this problem: disappointed in his own ability to solve it. She helped him formulate new targets for his company, and inspired him to involve others and not push himself to try and solve every problem on his own.

It's essential in influencing to:

- have a good assessment of the situation
- have a combination of focus on people as well as on targets/results
- be a partner to your clients in their quest, not a know-it-all.

These are the specific aspects that play a role in these examples:

- authenticity
- sincerity
- guts
- trusting the other person
- being inspired and having faith in the solutions
- enjoying the work, which will rub off on others.

Besides being able to assess the situation, it appears to be important to switch gears – from hard to soft, from showing empathy to having clarity about your own motives, and from being flexible in thinking along with the other person to being steady in what you want for yourself.

Food for thought: who in your private life, or in public life, influences you? What skills does he or she use? Which of these skills would you like to be able to use?

In the next chapters I will focus some more on what I call 'the four secrets for influencing effectively':

1 Determine the context/situation in which you want to influence, then your goal, and then your strategy.
2 Choose the influencing skill that fits your goal best.
3 Use this skill as consistently as you can.
4 Work on your ability to change gears and switch between the ten influencing skills.

3

Strategic choices

> *Three steps to heaven.*
>
> Eddie Cochran

If you do not think about your goal and your strategy when you want to influence others, there is a big risk that you will act on automatic pilot and do what you instinctively always do. Concentrating on what it is that you want to achieve will force you to make a more conscious decision about what behaviour will be the most effective in a particular situation that requires a specific strategy. In Chapter 4, you will find a description of a particular situation for every one of the ten influencing skills.

Here are a few examples of strategic questions you can ask yourself before choosing one of the ten influencing skills:

- Which relationships/contacts do I want to influence in my network?
- How can influencing help me succeed when implementing new developments?
- What employee/manager behaviour do I want to influence?
- How can I put forward my advice in the best way? Do I need to profile myself or should I operate from the sidelines?
- How urgent is this issue for me?
- Do I need support or can I operate alone?

Before you can apply any of the ten influencing skills:

- you make an analysis of the context in which you work and the precise situation you are in, and
- you determine your goal(s).

It is important to avoid automatically using your preferred behaviour. The behaviour that you are inclined to use will become clear from the self-analysis questionnaire on page 18.

A strategic choice is essential when deciding between different behavioural (influencing) alternatives. The next step is to switch effectively between the various influencing skills. Tips for switching are taken up in Chapter 5.

Analysing the context and the situation

Before you decide which influencing skill you want to use, make an analysis of the context in which you work and also of the specific situation. Do you work in a company or for an organization in which technical know-how and logic are important? Then, there is a fair chance that the skills of 'reasoning' or 'taking a position' will be appreciated.

However, if your colleagues have heard your arguments over and over again and seem disinclined to co-operate, it may be time to 'outline an attractive future perspective'. That can be a surprising switch. However, if you are up against a very robust, outspoken person, it might work better if you adapt your language and dynamics and use 'profiling' as the appropriate skill.

Determine your goal

Apart from assessing the context and the specific situation, it is wise to realize what your goal is. Here are some examples:

- If urgency is self-evident or there is a pressing time factor, opt for 'taking a position' or 'reasoning'.
- If you have time and need support, opt for 'listening' and 'involving others'.
- If it is time to make clear what you stand for, and what your role is, opt for 'profiling'.
- If your goal is to generate new energy for a subject that has been argued over for too long already, opt for 'outlining an attractive future perspective'.

A network analysis may help you by determining your goal and by making a choice of one of the influencing skills.

Scope of influence: a network analysis

- Goal: to get a clear image of the influencing factors on a specific goal.
- First step: formulate the goal that you want to reach. Do this in activating sentences such as 'how can I make sure that I achieve…'
- Second step: make a mind map of all the (possible) people who might be involved in realizing your goal. You can do this as follows:
  - Draw the interrelationships on a piece of paper.
  - Indicate, per person, what his or her relevance is to your problem.
  - Is it as a decision-maker?
  - Is it as an influencer?
  - Is it as a member of an audience?
  - Is it as a doer?
  - Indicate the quality of these relationships with coloured arrows connecting these people as follows: red – no relationship established so far, hard to approach (conflicts, distance); orange – neutral, approachable, but hardly an established relationship as yet; green – easy access, good contacts, et cetera.
- Third step: Based on the analysis of this dynamic field you draw conclusions and consider follow-up actions:
  - Improve the relationship.
  - Anticipate possible conflicts.
  - External communication.
  - Build (informal) meeting structures.

Self-analysis questionnaire

> *I did it my way.*
>
> Frank Sinatra

Which influencing skills do you usually use and which skills do you use less often? The following self-analysis test will help make this clear.

Circle the number in the questionnaire that typically describes your behaviour in the statement, where:
1 = never
2 = occasionally, less than average
3 = regularly, average (as often as other people)
4 = often, more than average
5 = always, nearly always

QUESTIONNAIRE

TP	I express my opinion clearly without directly anticipating the reactions.	1 2 3 4 5
R	I come up with counter-arguments if there are differences in opinion.	1 2 3 4 5
LS	I am an understanding listener if someone expresses feelings of, for example, anger/disappointment, happiness or sorrow.	1 2 3 4 5
GC	If I appreciate someone's contribution, I say so clearly.	1 2 3 4 5
P	I think it is useful to express my views and see what happens.	1 2 3 4 5
I	I use other people's contributions, even if their opinions differ from mine.	1 2 3 4 5
GR	I make a point of thanking other people for their contribution.	1 2 3 4 5
O	I like to draw up a long-term, perfect scenario for the department.	1 2 3 4 5
Ls	I am inclined to keep asking more penetrating questions and do not easily accept the initial answer to a question.	1 2 3 4 5
R	I support my opinions by logical reasoning.	1 2 3 4 5
T	I encourage people to try out something concrete once they are enthusiastic about my idea.	1 2 3 4 5
R	I analyse illogical stories and come up with objections.	1 2 3 4 5
T	I can translate my dream scenario into practical steps.	1 2 3 4 5
P	It is important for me to make my role and position clear.	1 2 3 4 5
TP	I use words like 'must' and 'should'.	1 2 3 4 5
GC	I make a deliberate effort to mention other people's successes.	1 2 3 4 5
GR	If my team is celebrating a success, I mention other people's contributions.	1 2 3 4 5
I	I show my personal feelings, such as hope or fear, and ask about other people's feelings.	1 2 3 4 5
C	At work, I often appeal to people's values.	1 2 3 4 5
O	I encourage the feeling that we are facing a task together.	1 2 3 4 5
T	If there are changes, I instigate the first action in order to show that it will work.	1 2 3 4 5

C	I try to make disheartened people enthusiastic again by tapping into their enjoyment of their work.	1 2 3 4 5
P	If I ask someone for something, I say what they can expect from me.	1 2 3 4 5
LS	I check that I have understood people properly by summing up what they have just said.	1 2 3 4 5
I	I invite other people to think along with my problem and take their suggestions seriously.	1 2 3 4 5
GR	If there has been a success, I can sideline myself and let someone else score the goal.	1 2 3 4 5
TP	I tell everyone clearly what I expect of them.	1 2 3 4 5
C	I look for work objectives that everyone can relate to.	1 2 3 4 5
O	I use images and analogies to visualise my idea of the future.	1 2 3 4 5
GC	I like it if another person is motivated by my appreciation.	1 2 3 4 5

Add up the points for GC, P, TP, R, LS, I, GR, O, C and T, and multiply R by 3 to see in which influencing skills you score the highest.

	Type of question	Is related to ... (= skill)
1	GC	Giving compliments
2	P	Profiling
3	TP	Taking a position
4	R	Reasoning
5	LS	Listening, summarising and asking follow-up questions
6	I	Involving the other person
7	GR	Giving recognition to the other person
8	O	Outlining an attractive future perspective
9	C	Connecting with the other person's values
10	T	Taking the first step

If you group 1, 2 and 3 together (GC, P and TP) your score indicates a forceful kind of behaviour. If you score well on 4, the R (x 3), reasoning and argumentation is well developed. Scoring on 5, 6 and 7 (LS, I and GR) together show that you have room for aspects to do with the relationship besides the task orientation. Adding 8, 9 and 10, your focus is on inspiring others.

Whatever the outcome of this self-analysis is, there is no 'right' or 'wrong' because there are no right or wrong answers. It only shows your inclination towards a preferred behavioural style. The skills you use most come easily to you. It is also possible that the context in which you work requires these skills and, therefore, that they are the most appreciated – so you have a strong reason to use them. That does not imply that these skills are also the most effective in all circumstances. This book invites you to experiment with skills you do not automatically use, but which help you in showing more effective behaviour. Experiment and experience what difference it might make. I will regularly give suggestions on how to practise concrete behaviour.

Please remember that practise makes perfect – so even though it feels unnatural in the beginning, do not give up. Learning to show new behaviour is difficult and takes time. Compare it to learning to play an instrument or to drive a car... Remember how hard that was?

If you show new and different behaviour, and the effects are positive, then you will feel motivated to continue and repeat your experiments. In doing so, you will notice that your options increase, and therefore your influence will grow. If you are also ready to switch between skills at the right time and in the right place, you can only add to your increasing influence.

> *Tip:* You can ask someone else (a colleague, a manager, your partner) to fill in the questionnaire for you. To draw conclusions on the basis of your own analysis is sometimes too restricted. Besides, the perspective that other people have of your behaviour might be enlightening.

Look at the scores on the test. Which skills are most developed in you? Do you recognise the outcome? Are there any surprises?

Here's a suggestion: Think about an example where you were in a situation and used a particular skill that, in hindsight, was not effective. Which skill would have been more appropriate? Do you use a particular skill considerably less than other skills, while in fact your goal or the situation you are in requires the use of another skill? Which one is it? Do you know why you tend not to use this skill?

ABOUT LEARNING BEHAVIOURAL SKILLS

You cannot change someone's personality. You can learn new behaviour, but let's face it: it's not going to be easy. Old fixed patterns and automatic-pilot behaviour are deeply ingrained in us. Acquiring new skills takes time, a lot of effort and perseverance and, most of all, the will to enlarge your behavioural capabilities. The ten influencing skills are not a recipe for instant success. Communication is too complex for that. You will have to deal with disappointment as well. However, your reward will be that you will be more effective, and be effective more often, than you used to be. After many training sessions on Influencing Skills with participants, and after reviewing them with colleagues, I can safely say that many people have had successful experiences in applying the influencing skills, often much to their surprise. I sincerely hope that you too will be successful and that you will allow yourself some time to master these skills.

The way we learn is very individual. Some people learn by doing and evaluating afterwards. Others need to grasp the theory first before they want to experiment. Try to find the way that suits you.

Using a new behavioural skill for the first time feels awkward. Try wearing your watch on your other wrist for fifteen minutes. This might look simple, but most people tend to move the watch back to where it originally was. Allow yourself some time to get used to your new behaviour and do not expect to be able to change it overnight. Experiment until you feel that it comes more naturally to you.

> *Suggestion:* after having read this book, write down the answers to the questions in the questionnaire, formulate your learning goals and complete the questionnaire again after a few months. You can also check with the people around you: can they recognise any outcome? There might be a difference between your intention to influence and its actual effect. In other words, check whether your self-perception coincides with how others perceive your influencing behaviour. You will possibly get some feedback that reinforces the importance of your newly acquired influencing skills. It is also possible that you are already more influential than you thought.

4

The ten influencing skills

> *You're gonna reap just what you sow!*
>
> Lou Reed

The influencing model

In this chapter, you'll find an overview of the ten influencing skills, the dynamics behind them and how they are done. You will get answers to the following questions:

- What influencing skills are there?
- Which behaviour belongs to each skill?
- When do you put the 'I' at the centre of your focus and when the 'other'?
- What intensity lies behind the skills?

I have placed these aspects in a model: the Influencing Model (page 23). It helps to place the skills in a logical, comprehensible way. Below is an explanation of the model.

The process

The process is about communication between you and the other person. Communication is an art, as is influencing.

The focus

Departing from 'what I want' to 'what do others want/need?'

The intensity

Most intensive and powerful when expressing 'what I want' are the skills Complimenting, Profiling and Taking a position. The dynamics here can be called 'forceful encouragement'.

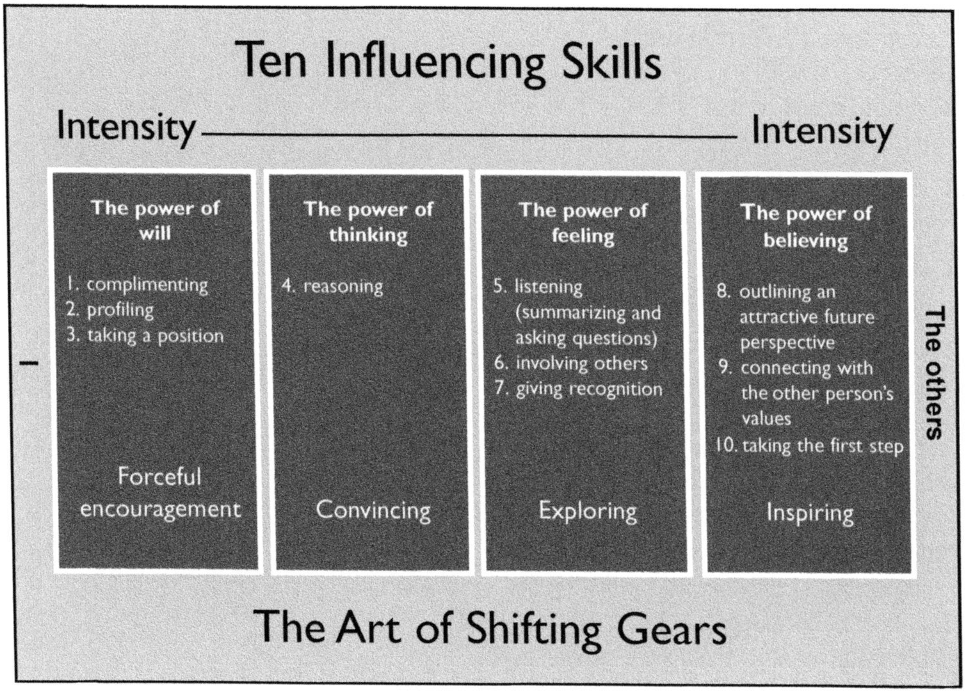

The intensity is a little less when I use Reasoning: still more focused on the task than on the relationship, but less coloured by personal norms and values than forceful encouragement, the dynamic here is 'convincing'.

The skills of Listening, Involving the other person and Giving recognition to the other person are also less intense but focus more on the relationship. The dynamic here is 'exploring.'

The intensity and power increases again when you Connect with the other person's values, Outline an attractive future perspective and indicate how you are going to Take the first step. Here there is a strong focus on the interest of other people rather than on the task itself. The dynamic here is inspiration.

Both your goal and the situation in which you operate determine how intensely you want to influence others and what dynamics you are going to use. In other words, how much room do you allow yourself and how much room is there for the other party?

The power that you use
The power of will, the power of thinking, the power of feeling and the power of believing are the sources you use to have influence.

A summary of the ten influencing skills:

The power of will:

1 Giving compliments
2 Profiling
3 Taking a position

What you do is: forceful encouragement, in an assertive approach

The power of thinking:

4 Reasoning

What you do is: convince, in a persuading approach

The power of feeling:

5 Listening (summarising and asking questions)
6 Involving others
7 Giving recognition to the other party

What you do is: explore, in an involving approach

The power of believing:

8 Outlining an attractive future perspective
9 Connecting with the other person's values
10 Taking the first step

What you do is: inspire, in an inspiring approach.

The following points describe each of the ten influencing skills – both the goal you want to achieve with the skill and what you actually say or do when using this particular influencing skill.

The power of will

1 COMPLIMENTING

> *You are everything and everything is you.*
>
> Marvin Gaye and Diana Ross

Goal

The other person feels supported by your compliment and feels motivated to show this desired behaviour again.

Situation
The issue at hand is of great importance to you. What you want is leading here and you put a lot of energy into it. The compliment is real and sincere.

The pitfall when giving compliments is that if you overload people with compliments or do it too often, they might start to feel uncomfortable. Even though it is a powerful and positive instrument, do not over-use it.

Behaviour
Motivate, emphasise what people are good at doing.

In general, giving a compliment is most powerful when it is meant as a true compliment, one without a hidden agenda on your part. In the context of effective behaviour, you therefore focus on the desired effects when you give compliments strategically. Mind you, it's important that the compliment is sincere and not just a trick.

> Food for thought: Think back to a situation in which you received a true compliment. What effect did it have on you?

Let's remember not to be stingy with giving compliments; they are not only a warm and pleasant way to influence each other, but also truly build credit in working relationships.

To give compliments

Northern Europeans in particular sometimes have a reputation for being reluctant to give compliments. Some managers tell their employees that they get paid to do their jobs well and that they will get feedback if they do not perform according to the company standards (read: will be criticised or reprimanded). These managers should not be surprised if their employees start complaining after some time that they are only getting negative feedback. Obviously, this is not motivating at all. You have missed the opportunity to influence here, to reward and appreciate an employee. It is almost impossible to overestimate the effect of complimenting.

To receive compliments

Compliment: 'That is an excellent piece of work. Very well done!'
Response: 'Oh, it was nothing, really.'

Another compliment: 'That's a nice suit you're wearing.'
Response: 'Oh, it was on sale and I got it really cheaply.'

Do you recognise these? This behaviour looks like genuine modesty but in fact you are rejecting the compliment and – implicitly – also its giver. People often tend to explain themselves after having received a compliment. When you do this the effect, however, is that you do not seem grateful. And that is exactly what you are supposed to be: grateful. Just say 'thank you'.

A compliment is a gift. Unwrap it and be grateful. Allow the giver of the compliment their moment and you influence them. Show your gratitude for the compliment and the person giving it.

It can be a strategic choice to give a compliment if you want an employee to continue showing the behaviour that you appreciate: 'It was fantastic, the way you dealt with that project last year!' This also reveals that you have faith in the employee which encourages and motivates. You hope that the message comes across and might add 'It would be wonderful if you took the responsibility for another such project'. You say it in a forcefully encouraging way because you would rather not start a discussion or hear objections. Non-verbally, you show that you are taking it for granted that the employee will go for it; do not wait for an answer. If he or she feels motivated to do the task, and is prepared to put aside objections (if any), you have reached your goal. In the case of serious objections, you have to switch to a more involving approach by listening and asking questions to find out the nature of the objections and explore what the employee needs to take up the project anyway.

> Example: 'How you managed that project last year was really top quality. You have motivated the project members, you met all the deadlines and the presentation of your end results was truly inspiring: there is only one person here that can do that and that's you!'

> Food for thought: Over the next two weeks, give at least three compliments to three different people and observe the effect on them. Also, give a compliment with the aim of encouraging the other person to display the behaviour that you appreciate again. See if that works for you. If you give a compliment, how does that affect you? And what are the effects on the other person?

2 PROFILING

> *True colours...*
>
> Cyndi Lauper

Goal
Others cannot ignore your strong profile and are persuaded.

Situation
It is urgent and important for you to show your true colours (your capabilities, norms and values) and demonstrate that you have a clear, firm profile.

Potential pitfalls when profiling yourself too strongly are that you reveal an inflated ego and talk down to people as if you were up in an ivory tower. You emphasize your knowledge and experience to such an extent that you come over as a know-it-all. Other people feel there's little room for them to take their own decisions and fear that you are underestimating the situation or the effects on them.

Behaviour
Show who you are and what you stand for. Research has shown that this leads to behaviour fit for managers. For a consultant, too, it is not only necessary to formulate significant questions but also to show:

- that you have ideas and opinions of your own
- that you undertake action based on your analysis
- that you can reach goals based on your convictions, and
- that you have a clear perception of your role.

> Examples: 'I have listened carefully to your plans for the reorganisation and, based on my experience and convictions, I have to admit that this is not the right approach: it is essential to involve your stakeholders in drawing up plans.'

Al Gore has stepped out of his own shadow by profiling himself as the advocate for improving our environment by making his film *An Inconvenient Truth*.

> Food for thought: For your next meeting, prepare a point on the agenda that is really important to you. Show the members of the meeting your expertise and knowledge. Try this on a friend or partner and ask for feedback on how strongly you come across in profiling yourself in this way. After the meeting, look back on the effects. Did you reach what you wanted to reach?

3 TAKING A POSITION

> *But if you go carrying pictures of chairman Mao you ain't gonna make it with anyone anyhow.*
>
> The Beatles

Goal
By taking a position in an assertive way, you make the other person change their position. Mind you, this is not the same as taking a stand and supporting it with arguments. That will be discussed in the next section on Reasoning.

Situation
Here it is important that you are firm in taking a position – for example, because people tend to like you, but do not always really hear what you have to say.

The pitfall is that if you do this too forcefully you might seem rigid and inflexible. People generally then feel resistance and respond with a 'no' whatever your proposal.

Behaviour
You take a (firm) position and do not want people to discuss or start a debate on the issue. Often, taking a position is confused with Reasoning (see the next point). When you reason and use arguments to convince or persuade the other party, you welcome your opponent's counter-argument because you need it to sharpen your ideas. When you choose to take a position, you do not want to hear counter-arguments. You want the other party to do what you want through the force of your willpower. The language you use in this approach is clear and firm:

- 'Experience has taught me ... and that's confirmed by research.'
- 'Absolutely!'
- 'No doubt about it!'
- 'I refuse to let this happen!'
- 'If we don't do it now, the project will fail!'
- 'This is what our target group wants.'

Example: In a meeting, you feel that your colleagues are tending to opt for Plan A. This would mean defeat for you because you are opting for Plan B. Arguments have been put on the table, and simply repeating all the arguments is useless. It is time to take a firm position: 'Plan A will be an absolute disaster, we can only reach our goals by implementing Plan B. And we have to do it now.'

Food for thought: Force yourself to take a position on an issue and refrain from giving arguments or explaining yourself. There will be a moment of silence after you do that. Simply wait for the reactions. If none are given, ask for one. It can feel awkward to take a position like this, so if you want to do it, prepare yourself mentally. Ask for feedback afterwards. What was the effect of your action on the other people? And what effect did it have on you?

These first three points dealt with the skills Complimenting, Profiling and Taking a position. They are grouped together in the Asserting Approach.

The power of thinking

4 REASONING

> *Reason to believe…*
>
> Tim Hardin

Goal

The other party feels persuaded to move in your direction despite their own point of view because they are convinced by your arguments. If not completely convinced, they will take your arguments seriously and take your points of view into consideration.

> *Empirical research has shown that arguments in a debate are effective when they are brought forward with audacity, clarity and resolve.*
>
> Dutch journalist Paul Witteman

According to clients and participants in our educational training, this statement is true. No doubt the power of thinking, the rational mind, is the key in this approach, but it means more than just being a sharp debater. You can win a debate if you present the sharpest arguments, but apparently the debater as an individual also plays an important role. If you believe in what you say it has more impact than if you argue for the sake of arguing. Authenticity is more important than being quick-witted. In your work environment, there is no room for behaving as though you were indulging in a recreational debate. Besides having good, logical arguments, it is also valuable to maintain good relationships. Nevertheless, the art of good argumentation can enhance your influence.

Situation

You work in an organisation in which logical argumentation and persuading based on reason is valued highly; this is often the case in a scientific or technical environment. Your proposal is not accepted just because you are pleasant to work with; you will have to argue decently and thoroughly to convince others and reach your goal.

A pitfall when reasoning is to generate too many arguments or to keep repeating the same ones. Often, people focus on the content too much and lose perspective on the dynamics in the interaction, the communication between them and the other person – for example, listening behaviour or resistance by the other person.

Behaviour

In the organisational context as described above, discussions are welcome, even necessary, to persuade others. So you come up with logical arguments and oppose the arguments of other people. You present facts and figures, repeat your message, provoke responses and show a focus on your goals.

> Example: 'My major arguments for introducing result-oriented management are these. First: the need to define clear and specific targets. Second: to encourage the personal development of our employees; I will return to this later. Also, I think it's important that we are clear on the agreements we make, both on a team as well as on an individual level, because it helps us to be clear on task descriptions. What's more, these agreements will contribute to our overall motivation. If people commit to mutual agreements they bear the responsibility, and will feel obliged to be proactive when they anticipate that they won't be able to meet expectations. Then there's still time to offer coaching as a means to help them meet their expectations and realize their (company) goals after all. So, in order to grow as an organisation, I think it's essential to make agreements on results as well as invest in personal development.'

Analysing what the speaker does here:

- he or she presents the two strongest arguments
- in the middle, a few more are offered
- and the speech concludes with the two arguments that are personally the most important.

Effective reasoning

Some more tips for effective reasoning:

- Start by giving your two or three most powerful arguments, then follow them with others, but close again with the two or three arguments you used in your opening. They will stick.
- It helps when you support your arguments non-verbally, perhaps by counting them on your fingers, and have a firm physical presence.

- Argue firmly, but do not become rigid and inflexible.
- Show that you have looked at the issue from several angles.
- Admit it when the other party scores a point: 'You have a point there, but let me show you another side…'
- You consciously respond to the other person's arguments – firstly, because you do not want to cling to your own frame of reference; secondly, to show flexibility in the debate from arguing to counter-arguing.
- Use arguments, not knives.
- Separate people from issues.
- Take the floor but also give room to the other person.
- Explain yourself or your arguments if necessary.
- Focus on what is actually being said, not on your own interpretation of it.
- If you hear a false line of argument, mention it.

Reasoning in the context of work

At work, when you are confronted with a difference of opinion and you want to discuss this, you may want to win the argument, but you also want to retain a good working relationship. It is not effective if you completely over-power the other person. Preferably, consider the following professional way of structuring your confrontation:

Confrontation

You establish the fact that there are differences of opinion and come to an agreement about the way you want to exchange arguments with your opponent.

Opening

Make clear that you are going to argue the pros or the cons. It is more acceptable if you are open about it and say things like 'Do you mind me playing the devil's advocate on this?' or 'Do you mind if I show you the other side of this argument?' The effect will be that you create a psychological contract on your intention to explore the pros and cons instead of seeking a personal attack.

Reasoning

You exchange your arguments, using the tips mentioned above.

Closure

Make sure you agree on the outcome of the discussion. Ask check questions, not on the content, but on the process. For example:

- What did this exchange of arguments amount to?
- Where do we stand?
- How can we proceed, knowing where we stand?

Using this structure, you can argue firmly while at the same time you keep the working relation intact.

Differences between reasoning and debating: Roderik van Grieken, CEO of the Dutch Debating Institute in Hilversum, says 'The goal when debating, other than when arguing, is truth-finding. Reasoning in an organisational context is used to exchange opinions and ideas to come to well-balanced decisions.'

> Food for thought: Argue your opinion on a current topic to a friend, using the tips mentioned above. Ask for feedback on how effective you were. What was good and what points for improvement are there?

When reasoning, you try to persuade or convince the other party by using (rational) arguments. Unlike the assertive approach, you invite discussion, even if this is only done for the sake of being able to counter-argue.

The power of feeling

5 LISTENING, SUMMARISING AND ASKING FOLLOW-UP QUESTIONS

> *Come talk to me.*
>
> Peter Gabriel

Note: from here on, Listening, summarising and asking follow-up questions will generally be abbreviated to LSQ...

Goal
To give the other person the feeling that you are sincerely interested in them, which often leads to the other person being interested in your ideas and motivation.

Situation
You need the other party to create consensus. It is therefore essential to know what's on the other person's mind and in their heart. You have influence when you are truly interested in the other person.

The pitfall when using the power of feeling is to exaggerate empathy and lose yourself in the other party's experience, instead of switching to your own opinions and feelings.

Behaviour

You place the other party at centre stage and make an effort to find out what is important and of value to them. You pose questions from a position of genuine interest.

Listening

Active listening entails a lot. It is an attitude which means opening yourself up to the other person and being curious. Non-verbally, you show active listening by establishing eye contact, nodding and humming ('hmm-hmm') to encourage the other person in telling their story. You show that your attention is focused on them and that you have time to listen. You do not interrupt; you do not 'steal' the story by saying that you recognise it and then taking over. The other person remains centre stage.

Summarising

You can greatly influence a conversation by giving a good summary and then asking follow-up questions. Summarising has two functions:

- checking: 'Did I understand you correctly?'
- directing: 'If I understand you correctly, you're mentioning three issues. I would like to know more about the second one.' Here, you are already asking the follow-up question.

Follow-up questions

Just like a journalist, you ask follow-up questions because you want to know everything. Your attitude is one of genuine curiosity. You might say 'I get it' but (non-verbally) the message is 'tell me more'.

> Example: 'I have the idea that you're not thrilled about this proposal. Is that correct?' If this is confirmed, then 'Can you tell me why not, or explain your objections?' After getting the answer, 'Right, I understand what you mean and can imagine why. What can I do to remove your objections?'

> Food for thought: Practise LSQ in your private life. Observe what the effects are. Do you get more information than you expected? Does the other person reveal more than you hoped for? If so, you are using LSQ effectively.

Watch an interview on television with this LSQ focus and monitor the interviewer. When do they do a good LSQ job, and when not? What are the effects on the interviewee? Also watch out for the effect of closed questions (yes/no questions); usually they do not gain a lot of information. Please realize that this is a complex skill and take some comfort in the fact that there is room for improvement – even for professional interviewers.

6 INVOLVING THE OTHER PERSON

> *Ik kan het niet alleen.*
> (I cannot do it on my own.)
>
> De Dijk

Goal
You want to invite the other person to contribute because you need their knowledge and/or commitment to reach a consensus.

The pitfall when involving others is not being clear as to who takes the final decision.

Situation
As a manager you are asked by your superior to implement a particular procedure. You are sure that your employees will object to it because they cannot see its merits and also because it will take up valuable time. It is impossible for you to refuse this assignment but you are afraid that your employees will do so. You involve them in this problem by being honest and saying that you are not happy either, and ask them to think about the questions of what this implementation might bring in terms of advantages for your department, and what possibilities can be seen when you do implement the procedure.

Behaviour
You explain your dilemma and invite the others to respond to this. You ask the other people to co-create and sum up the pros and cons. You openly appreciate their contribution and take their ideas seriously. You can even put the issue on the table and say that you do not have the solutions, thus making the other people co-owners of the problem. You can even give the others an important role in the decision-making process.

When you realize that you cannot solve the problem on your own, you can influence others by giving them a true sense of co-operation. You trust the other people, and one possible effect of that is that they trust you in return, or at least feel flattered that you value their opinion and/or assessment of the situation.

> Examples: 'I've come a long way in writing this report but I think it's important that you also have a good look at it and add your ideas. After all, you have to work with it, so you're entitled to influence it by sharing your ideas. Also, I have to admit that I'm not 100% sure about this. Think along with me here.'

By disclosing a problem or dilemma you have, you invite a response from the other person: 'I understand the problem; to be quite honest, I was also wondering about it...' or

'Now that you are being so honest about it, I must admit that I can also see the positive side of it' or maybe 'I would get extremely nervous if that happened. Do you see that?'

> Food for thought: If you are inclined to withdraw and wrestle with difficult issues on your own, experiment and share your inner struggle with someone close to you. With your next (business) plan or project, force yourself to share your ideas with a colleague before you finalise the plan. Be aware of the effect that it has on the other party; you can ask them afterwards what being involved by you meant to them.

7 GIVING RECOGNITION TO THE OTHER PERSON

> *This is a man's world, but it would have been nothing without a woman or a girl.*
>
> James Brown

Goal
To feed self-esteem in other people and make them feel important, so that they are willing to see it your way.

Situation
After involving another person by looking into a problem or an issue together, you show recognition for their contribution.

The pitfall when giving recognition is that you profile yourself too little. You value the other person too much and minimise your own contribution.

Behaviour
You give credit to the other person's contribution. If people get the feeling that they are important and that their contribution counts, it often leads to commitment – and therefore your influence increases. You reward and recognise the other party's contribution to your goals by explicitly thanking them for:

- thinking along
- the suggestions they have made
- the commitment shown
- the critical questions, if any, that they have raised.

> Example: 'Thank you for your part in writing this plan. You have been able to make these plans far more applicable and practical than I could have done. I suggest we include your name on this as co-author.'

> Food for thought: Pay attention this month to the positive contributions people make that go beyond what is expected of them. Do not take them for granted (as you usually do?), but explicitly mention the contribution and your appreciation of it. Of course, you will pay attention to the effect this has on the other person.

What you are doing when you use the influencing skills Listening, summarising and asking follow-up questions (point 5), Involving the other person (point 6) and Giving recognition to the other person (point 7) is exploring all possible actions in terms of co-operation. Whereas your will and thinking power is more task-oriented, the power of feeling is central here, and is relationship-oriented. Empathy is the key.

The power of believing

8 OUTLINE AN ATTRACTIVE FUTURE PERSPECTIVE

> *Somewhere, over the rainbow, way up high,*
> *there's a land that I dreamed of, once in a lullaby.*
>
> *Rufus Wainwright*

Goal
Generate new energy by taking others along in your vision of the future on a realistic route, while at the same time showing the first concrete step to be taken.

Situation
You have done everything you can to reach your goal but it seems as if the other party is tiring of the subject; all the arguments are well known. Daily pressure leads to tunnel vision and it seems impossible to think in the long term. What is necessary now is new energy – by influencing in a surprisingly fresh way.

The pitfall when outlining an attractive future perspective is that you can lose your perspective on reality and become impractical.

Behaviour
Outline an attractive future perspective and paint a picture of a situation you really believe in. Use a metaphor, give an example, cite a parallel, paint a picture. A picture says more than a thousand words and is easier to remember than words alone.

Link this future perspective to the interests of others. People only start to move when they believe that there is something in it for them. Then let others take the first step – after you have shown what the first step to realizing the dream could be.

The renowned management guru John P. Kotter supports this approach. In his book *Leading Change* he describes the importance of having a vision and believing in it, in communicating it and in generating a short-term success.

> Examples: 'This morning, when I was on the train I got this idea: our HR department will change from a leading department to a more consulting department in a year. Instead of writing and improving policy on paper, we will offer our clients – because that's what our colleague departments are – useful information and the methods and means that they need.'

Or think about the legendary words by Martin Luther King – 'I have a dream' – and Barack Obama's 'What we need is hope and change.'

> Food for thought: Leave the work pressure where it is for a moment. Try to avoid thinking in problems but visualise what the ideal situation might look like in a year.

9 CONNECTING WITH THE OTHER PERSON'S VALUES

> *Baby, you can sleep while I drive.*
>
> Melissa Etheridge

Goal

The other party shares your vision because they can see what is in it for them.

Situation

You have been inspiring in communicating your vision. People start to get enthusiastic. Now it is important to feed enthusiasm and translate it into action. That will only succeed when others see that your vision is really profitable for them.

The pitfall when connecting with others is that you identify with their interests to such an extent that you lose sight of the overall vision.

Behaviour
To avoid the cynical attitude of people saying 'dream on' and disconnecting themselves, you have to make it crystal clear what the interests of other people are when working on your future perspective. Keep 'what's in it for them' in mind.

> Example: If you know that your team values co-creation and innovation highly, make sure that you mention these elements explicitly in your inspiring presentation.
>
> Food for thought: Put yourself in the other person's shoes – what would be important to you and inspire you to start moving?

10 TAKING THE FIRST STEP

> *I'm walking!*
>
> Fats Domino

Goal
Generate a short-term success and give the other party the feeling that they can truly contribute to your vision, and also have the power to influence it.

After having taken the first step, Kotter argues that it is of great importance to reward new and effective behaviour. In the eight steps he describes in *Leading Change*, the goal of making the first concrete step is to generate a short-term success. People start to believe that the idea can work. Giving recognition and Involving the other person also help.

It goes without saying that the intention when using this influencing style is that you motivate people to show this effective behaviour again, just as in Complimenting (page 24). It's not just about people following your dream; it's also about being able to sketch a realistic route. Knowing the nature of the first step is a condition for beginning to believe that the goal is attainable.

Situation
You see enthusiasm in the other party because of your vision. They see the advantages in embracing your future perspective. It is important now to move on and put your money where your mouth is: take a first concrete step to prove that your dream will work.

The pitfall when taking the first step is to be too hasty and drown in practicalities, thus losing your perspective on the dream, the end goal.

Behaviour

To make sure that your dream is experienced as realistic, desirable and attainable it is necessary that your audience is clear on the first step to take. This is exactly what Kotter calls essential too: generate a short-term success. The behaviour that has made taking the first step possible, and which might even have led to the first real success, has to be rewarded. It will provoke the same kind of successful behaviour.

> Example: We are inspired by the government to use energy-saving light bulbs as a first step on our way to addressing the planet's serious environmental problems. The reward is that we feel we have contributed to a world-wide problem, instead of feeling powerless in facing such an immense task.

> Food for thought: The power of believing and the inspiring approach have been described in point 8 (Outlining an attractive future perspective), in point 9 (Connecting with the other person's values) and point 10 (Taking the first step).

Think of a goal that you want to reach, one where you realize that others might not be too open to your ideas – for example, because too many arguments have already been exchanged. Try to present your goal with these four elements:

1 Outline an attractive future perspective.
2 Use a metaphor or paint a picture.
3 Connect to their values.
4 Make clear which step can already be taken.

It's essential here that you absolutely believe in this future goal. Paint your picture and do not allow interruptions by discussion. Try to generate new energy for the subject.

There are two secrets to using all of the skills mentioned effectively:

1 If you use a skill, be consistent and use it purely: do not mix styles initially.
2 If you use a skill and it does not have the desired effect, switch to another style.

Last but not least: Do nothing.

> *Let it be.*
>
> The Beatles

There are ten influencing skills, but there is one more option: do nothing.

DO NOTHING

Sometimes you influence a situation by not using any of the skills but by making a strategic choice to do nothing. Silence can be powerful and some situations do not require action. So you do not do anything – but you *do* make a conscious choice to Do Nothing.

Situation

- There is too much tension, the negotiations are at a dead end, the time is not ripe yet.
- It is high time that you put your ego aside and gave the floor to another person.
- You want to show that you are flexible enough to give up one of your points (maybe to score later on, on another subject).

Behaviour

- You remain silent…
- You go away…
- You avoid the conflict…
- You change the subject…
- You use humour…
- You give the floor to someone else.

Example: 'I'm getting the feeling that this isn't making you happy. You know what I'll do? I'll withdraw my proposal. Let's get some coffee.'

Food for thought: If you find yourself getting over-agitated or too fanatic about the subject, ask yourself whether it is really worth your while. Is doing nothing an option? And is it, maybe, much better than pushing the point any further?

Switching between the ten influencing skills

If you feel that an influencing skill is not being effective, do not persist in using it but switch to another skill – one that works.

This sounds easier than it actually is, because first you have to be aware that the skill you are using is ineffective. That implies a raised level of consciousness and self-awareness. It is complex to move from empathy to taking a position, from arguments to inspiration and back. In one conversation, in one meeting, you switch skills in minutes, sometimes even seconds, in order to be effective. This is a form of communication excellence that you can learn, but it takes time and a lot of effort.

Here are some examples.

1 'In my opinion we must raise our budget for this project!' Taking such a strong stand has a counter-effect on the general manager, who immediately resists the idea. You switch to Listening, summarising and asking follow-up questions: 'Under what conditions would you be tempted to consider this proposal?'

2 The other way around can also be effective: you start with a question, but if you notice that the other person is not particularly excited, you switch to Outlining an attractive future perspective: 'Imagine that this project generates more income and more company pride in six months…'

3 A fairly common situation: you Take a position. You notice that it has an influence, but more is required. You switch to Reasoning because you feel that logic and arguments are necessary to convince the other person.
Position: 'This project is definitely going to generate more revenue.'
Arguments: 'Our clients are asking for this product, our colleagues cannot wait to start offering it and, what is more, we're beating the competitor because we're the first on the market with this development.'

4 Option 2: you start by Outlining an attractive future perspective. You feel that it generates energy but some people are still sceptical and need more, so you switch to Taking a (firm) position. Perspective: 'Imagine this – in six months this project will generate more revenue, new customers and much more work satisfaction for our colleagues!' Position: 'If we do not do this, our competitors will!'

Food for thought: Think back on a business conversation or a negotiation in which you did not manage to influence the other party. In hindsight, can you see an opening now in which you could have switched to another influencing skill? In your next encounter, switch to another influencing skill at least once when you feel that you are not being effective enough with the one you are using.

5

The ability to switch gears while implementing a management style

> *It's half past four, and I'm shifting gear.*
>
> Golden Earring

The context

An organisation runs into the following problems:

- inadequate focus on goals and results
- not enough attention paid by management to the development of the company's human resources.

The board of directors has made the decision to introduce Result Oriented Management. Two elements are essential to this management style, and they are equally important:

1 Reaching concrete goals and specific targets
2 Developing independence and responsibility in employees.

Managers will have to devote time to realize this goal. They have to focus on the dialogue with their employees and make result-oriented agreements. They also have to plan and execute reviews and assessment talks. As this will take time, they will have to delegate more of their non-essential management tasks: their operational tasks. In order to do this, the employees will have to be independent and able to take on more responsibilities.

Actually, result-oriented *working* would be a better term because it reveals the process between managers and their employees, one in which they are interdependent. It is a condition that employees are also firmly committed to this concept. As it is hard, if not impossible, to demand commitment, managers need their influencing skills.

The next steps show which influencing skill may be most effective:

1 Translate the organisation's vision, mission and strategy into a personalised proposal for concrete goals on your department or unit level – i.e. use Profiling, Taking a position, Reasoning and Outlining an attractive future perspective.
2 Involve your team. Let them give you feedback on your presentation of the goals and invite them to add goals of their own – i.e. use LSQ, Involving others, Giving recognition, Complimenting and Connecting with the other person's values.
3 In the case of resistance, explain why changes are absolutely necessary – i.e. use an assertive approach in Taking a position but also Outlining an attractive future perspective, and give arguments.
4 Draw up agreements based on results with individual employees: 'Which contribution can you make towards reaching our goals as formulated in our year plan?' – i.e. use LSQ, Taking a position and Complimenting.
5 Make a point of what the employee's first concrete step can be – i.e. use Taking the first step.
6 Coach your employee in regular review meetings – i.e. use Involving the other person, LSQ and Outlining an attractive future perspective.

6

Influencing by middle management

> *Torn between two lovers…*
>
> Mary MacGregor

This chapter shows how you can use the ten influencing skills to make choices in the loyalty dilemma between your manager and your team.

The position of the manager as the link in middle management is probably the most interesting and fascinating position in an organisation – and also the most challenging position, one where you feel squeezed between your boss and your team. It is expected that you will be able to translate the vision, mission, strategy and the policies of the CEO, while at the same time representing your team and defending their interests to top management. You try to survive by empathy and understanding. However, empathy and translating top-down measures will not be enough by themselves. You are also expected to take a stand, to profile yourself in your management role and position.

This is what we call a loyalty problem.

Your loyalty is on the line, especially when tough nuts have to be cracked and the measures that have to be taken are not popular. You want to meet the interests of both your superiors and your team members.

Example: Despite the fact that you are under-staffed and experiencing a peak in the workload of your department, hiring temps is forbidden with immediate effect. Cutting costs is a legitimate reason. Therefore, your manager – having his or her own interests – expects you to execute this new measure forthwith and demands your loyalty to the company policy. Your team members, however, have their own expectations and interests: you ought to tell the management that the situation is getting out of hand and that they have reached their limits. What can you do? You cannot please them both.

The solution: You need to live up to your linking position and take responsibility in your role and position. This is a unique position: you know the background to the decision, and the reasons of your management, as well as the concerns of your team. You might be the only one to see this complex process for what it is. If you succeed in joining the expectations and interests of both parties or if you are able to come to an acceptable compromise, then you can show that your position has added value and that you are really living up to your position as a middle manager.

So, what you do is communicate what you see, the way you analyse the tensions and above all how you see the solution(s). This type of dilemma requires you to be firm and clear in what you stand for in your middle management position.

How to deal with influencing skills here?

The conclusion from the previous chapter is that you can only solve a loyalty problem between the interests of your boss and the interests of your team by influencing both parties. Let's see which influencing skill you can use in your communication with both your boss and your team and, at the same time, take a firm stand in your own role.

First, two pitfalls:

1 The yes-man. If you opt for blindly executing measures as your boss sees fit and not being critical at all, then your team will see you as a yes-man: someone with no mind of their own, no profile as such and no solidarity with their needs. Someone who is just there to execute decisions by higher management.
2 The shop steward. If you side with your team and only voice their interests, your boss will see you as effectively a shop steward or a member of the Works Council, someone who has lost their perspective on the nature of their position in the organisation.

Remember, these roles are important and valuable in their own context, so there is no judgment here – but as a middle manager you simply cannot afford to be a stool pigeon or a union rep: you have to take your own stand.

Therefore, if you have a loyalty problem – use your influencing skills!

Influencing skills when communicating with your manager and your team

In your specific role as a middle manager, it is especially relevant to influence your own manager and your own team in a transparent way. You do not have the formal power to halt any unpopular measure.

INFLUENCING OPTION 1

One option is to discuss with your fellow middle managers whether you, as a group, can convince top management of the negative effects of the measures they have announced. This might sound a little unusual because middle managers are not usually organised in the way a management team with pre-arranged meetings is organised. In my view, this is a pity because middle managers miss influencing opportunities. The influencing skills here are Reasoning and Outlining an attractive future perspective, one where the measures would not be implemented.

INFLUENCING OPTION 2

If you have to execute the unpopular measure anyway, you can still try to influence the way the measure will be implemented, and also the timing of its implementation.

Influencing your manager

Your manager's interest lies in a swift and efficient implementation of the measure concerned. Share your vision of the problems you foresee if you implement this measure in the way a yes-man would do it. Involve your boss and ask for a meeting in which you share your legitimate questions. In this way, you make your manager into a co-problem owner of the implementation, not because you are unwilling to implement the measure but because you are showing concern for its effectiveness. A meeting with your manager about this issue can contain the following elements:

- Is there still a possibility of influencing the content of the measure?
- Is there any time for team members to think along with it and offer solutions on the timetable for implementation?
- How do you deal with resistance in your team?
- What do you need yourself, as a middle manager, to make this implementation successful?

Finally, make sure you have analysed the issue well and discuss this analysis with your manager.

In short:

- Do not take the decision to execute the measure too hastily. Prevent a situation arising in which you have to implement a measure without having thought of alternative scenarios.
- Take the time to oversee the consequences of the implementation.
- Make it clear that you are being co-operative, but that there are consequences if you want to do it successfully.
- Involve your manager in thinking about the consequences.
- Ask relevant questions instead of only mentioning problems and objections.
- Discuss the positive as well as the negative effects of the measure.
- How can you deal with the negative effects?

Use these influencing skills on your manager: Taking a position, Involving the other person, Giving recognition, LSQ and Reasoning.

Influencing your team

In the same situation:

- Clarify the reasoning behind the measure and ask for your team's response.
- Make it clear that you realise the consequences. Be explicit in saying that you have discussed the pros and cons with your manager and that you have tried to influence him or her.
- Show your own colours, your own point of view, on this matter.
- Share which aspects you have been able to influence and which not.
- Show how you take your responsibility and how you think about the actual implementation.
- Ask your team members to give their ideas about the implementation: 'How do we cope with negative effects and what might work to our advantage?'
- Be curious and truly interested in your co-workers' ideas, opinions, wishes.
- Develop procedures for participation when far-reaching measures have to be taken.
- After adequate discussion, nip complaining behaviour in the bud and encourage making the first step together.

Use these influencing skills on your team: Reasoning, Profiling, Involving the other person, Giving recognition, Taking the first step.

It is essential to communicate your own involvement to both sides – not to protect yourself, but in order to be able to fulfil your role and position as a middle manager well. Your goal is to play a constructive role from your unique and specific position.

7

Influencing for consultants

> *Reach out; I'll be there.*
>
> The Four Tops

In this chapter I will link influencing skills to the consultant's behaviour, with a focus on the internal consultant.

The effective consultant has knowledge of:
- the different roles a consultant can have/play
- the phases in the process of consultancy
- the characteristics that make a consultant successful.

To be effective as a consultant, you need influencing skills. These are essential tools for the consultant's toolbox. Below you will find a description of the roles, the phases and the relevant characteristics as well as the most effective influencing skill.

Roles of the consultant

The role a consultant can play in an organisation is largely dependent on the client. The client might want to use the consultant's expertise as a specialist in their field – i.e. knowledge based. The client might also want to use the consultant as a partner in crime/twin partners, asking the consultant to operate and execute tasks just as the client would do. A very different client question would be if the consultant were asked to join the whole process and give input on content as well as on process. In other words, not just think along and give advice on the 'what' but also on the 'how'. In this case, the consultant's role is that of a partner.

Influencing skills per role

The client determines to a great extent what role the consultant is supposed to play. However, as a consultant you can also influence this decision and express what kind of role or roles you want to play. Although there's nothing wrong with the first two roles, the ideal role for consultants is to become partners. This role and position gives room for advice on different dimensions, and also about the role perception of the client and the responsibility that the client takes.

Here too, your focus is essential. What role do you want in this organisation? What is your goal? If you have made this decision, the influencing skills below will help you reach your goal:

- The expert: Profiling, Taking a position, Reasoning
- The partner in crime: Involving the other person, Giving recognition and Connecting with the other person's values
- The partner: Outlining an attractive future perspective, LSQ, Taking a position.

The consultancy process

As a consultant you take five steps in the consultancy process.

Phase 1:

The entry and contracting phase. Here you establish a relationship with your client and come to a (psychological) contract in which you also define your role as a consultant. In this initial phase, you can exert your influence on what role you want to fulfil.

If things go wrong in the consultancy process, more often than not it is because in the initial phase too little time was devoted to the entry and contracting phase. Especially when dealing with internal consultants, the client is tempted to skip this phase and just ask the consultant to get the job done. The assumption here is 'We know each other and you know what I want, don't you?' As an (internal) consultant it is your job to influence the situation in the initial phase and take time for this introductory and/or contract meeting.
Influencing skills in the entry and contract phase: LSQ and a little Profiling.

Phase 2:

Diagnose phase. Here you gather all the information you need to come to an analysis of the client's question.
Influencing skills in the diagnose phase: Reasoning, LSQ.

Phase 3:
Making a plan of action. This plan of action is based on your analysis and the recommendations you make as a consultant. This might be a tough phase because you also give feedback to your client, and on the organisation.
Influencing skills in the plan of action phase: Reasoning, Taking a position, Giving recognition, Involving the other and Connecting with the other person's values.

Phase 4:
The implementation. This phase involves the implementation of your recommendations, in which you also give advice and try to promote the desired behaviour necessary to make your points for improvement.
Influencing skills in the implementation phase: Involving the other person, Complimenting.

Phase 5:
The evaluation and closure phase. Together with your client, you look back on the successful steps that have been taken and also on the steps still to be taken. Based on your evaluation, it is decided to either come to a closure on the consultation or see whether follow-up steps are necessary. This phase is too often taken for granted when you are an internal consultant. Please try and influence your client to organise a meeting to discuss the evaluation and closure phase. You can also evaluate your role as a consultant, and the role of your client. Then you show real partnership.
Influencing skills in the evaluation and closure phase: Taking a position, LSQ.

Of course, the influencing skills mentioned here are suggestions. In our complex world in which communication is equally complex, you probably have to switch more often, or even use another skill. Unfortunately, there is no recipe book for all communicative encounters and as well as using all my tips, you have to trust your intuition too.

As a footnote to this chapter, let's consider the important competencies of the professional consultant.

Many consultants assume that their clients value their expert knowledge and quality the most. Research, however, shows that the client takes these competencies for granted and that they have other preferences. It may be interesting to note that clients have these as the top five most important competencies for consultants:

1 A good balance between task and relationship orientation.
2 A good combination of empathy and detachment, being objective.
3 An ability for self-reflection and dealing with uncertainty.
4 Entrepreneurship and proactivity.
5 Creativity.

The added value of the internal consultant:
A lot has been said and written about the disadvantages of the internal consultant compared to the external consultant (see the Bibliography). To support the internal consultant, I will list advantages that give internal consultants their added value:

- The internal consultant can be proactive.
- The internal consultant is there when any recommendations are implemented
- and can therefore be proactive again.

In order to live up to this added value, internal consultants have to profile themselves. They have to prove that they are able to deal with complex matters and have a helicopter view of the organisation. Despite the fact that they are part of the political system in the organisation, they have to take a firm position and be able to outline an attractive future perspective. Only then will they be seen as independent consultants, a true match for external ones.

It is important to sit down and 'sign' the psychological contract with your client prior to accepting the task. Be explicit and ask whether playing the devil's advocate will be appreciated.

In short, internal consultants will have to fight for the position external consultants already have because their title automatically gives them authority. It goes without saying that influencing skills will help you to gain this position when you talk about your psychological contract.

8
Influencing yourself and influencing resistance in others

Open the windows of your mind.

Jan Bijker, in *Breathtaking*

Influencing yourself

There is a fair chance that you feel an inner resistance to using one or more of the influencing skills. Human functioning comes from thoughts, feelings and behaviour. These are intertwined and thoughts and beliefs greatly influence our feelings and our behaviour. Also, as most of our behaviour is fixed in patterns, new behaviour feels awkward. Rational Emotive Therapy (RET) is a cognitive behavioural therapy and also a training method for finding out whether your thoughts and beliefs are rational or irrational. If they are irrational, you can look for more productive thoughts because these will help you be more effective in your behaviour.

This chapter just hints at the possibilities of transforming irrational into rational thoughts and therefore becoming a more effective professional, but for further reading I refer to *The Stumbling Blocks of the Mind*.

INTERNAL RESISTANCE

The internal resistance you might feel when you want to apply new skills need not be a problem. It's only when it becomes too much that it undermines your effective behaviour. In the following examples, the thoughts are rather black and white, but remember that internal resistance and unproductive thoughts go deeper than you might think. In the examples below there is a possible unproductive thought after mentioning each skill.

Examples:

- Giving compliments: 'They'll think I'm sucking up.'
- Profiling: 'They must think, "what a blown-up ego, how arrogant".'
- Taking a position: 'Who am I to say such a thing?'
- Reasoning: 'I will not be a smart arse and look like a politician...'
- LSQ: 'I'm not going for a degree in journalism! I just want to say what I think!'
- Involving the other person: 'People always misuse this.'
- Giving recognition to the other person: 'I'd better not! They will ask for a raise if I give them a reason...'
- Outlining an attractive future perspective: 'They will think that I have my head in the clouds and won't take me seriously anymore.'
- Connecting to the other person: 'Humpf, I'm not a wimp, let people take care of themselves!'
- Taking the first step: 'I am the only one who can do it properly, you can't leave it to others.'

If these thoughts prevent you from showing new behaviour, it's a pity. You can see from these examples how definite and fixed these thoughts are and, therefore, also how hard to change. True, it requires self-reflection and the willpower to do something about it, and also the guts to question your own thoughts. The next step would be to transform the unproductive thoughts into more productive ones, a coping statement like 'What can I say to myself the moment I am aware that I am thinking unproductive thoughts?'

RATIONAL EFFECTIVENESS TRAINING

RET is a cognitive behavioural approach and works from the conviction that our thoughts influence our emotions and therefore our behaviour. Obviously, if these thoughts are positive and generate energy there is no problem whatsoever. But if our thoughts are unproductive, our behaviour will be ineffective. It is therefore worthwhile trying to influence these thoughts and turn them into productive, helpful thoughts instead. This is not magic and certainly not easy to do, but it is a scientifically proven method for helping people to become more productive and more effective in their behaviour.

Influencing resistance in others

There is a fair chance that you will meet with resistance from your manager and/or your team. How can you use the influencing skills when this happens?

Realize these:

1 Great, there's resistance!
  The reflex response to resistance is that it is a nuisance and difficult to deal with, but realize that showing resistance is also a form of communication. It is therefore easier to influence resistance than the situation which develops when people start complaining amongst themselves while you are not around to pick up what is going on. Try to resist your reflex response that resistance is difficult to deal with, and find an opportunity to influence the resistance effectively.
2 Look out for the boomerang effect.
  Resistance requires serious attention to prevent it from going underground and surfacing again unexpectedly. Therefore you need to give resistance adequate attention and help people express their objections.

Especially when it comes to organisational changes, people need a transition phase to be able to leave behind the old (working) situation and accept the new one. Even though the new situation might not be dramatically different in your eyes, it might be for them. Explore the nature of their worries and complaints, and help them to blow off steam. Allow them some time to adapt to the new situation.

The influencing skills you need here are LSQ, Involving the other person, Giving recognition, Connecting with the other person's values, Outlining an attractive future perspective and Taking the first step.

9
Finally...

> *And in the end, the love you take is equal to the love you make...*
>
> The Beatles

After having read this book, you can start increasing your behavioural capacities. You will be able to use new influencing skills, or use those influencing skills that you would not automatically select but can choose now that you are more aware of what might be more effective.

Allow yourself some learning space; experiment with new behaviour. Hopefully, this book will have helped you to gain an insight into the process of influencing so that you can choose different behaviour. Depending on your goal and the specific situation, you can make a strategic choice out of the ten influencing skills.

In the Netherlands, we offer training sessions to all kinds of professionals, consultants and managers to allow them to become aware of their own style and to experiment with and apply (new) influencing skills. It is our ambition to be able to offer this in other countries as well. We also want to be able to offer this book in English for our international clients, hence this translation.

Finally, I'd also like to share my personal opinions about effective influencing:

- If you want to use an influencing skill, it is necessary to be aware of the situation you are in and also have a clear idea about your goal.
- Based on the assessment of the situation and on your goal, make a conscious choice of one of the ten influencing skills.
- Essential to this choice is whether you want to use the power of will, the power of thinking, the power of feeling or the power of believing.
- If you manage to use the ten influencing skills you can switch from one to the other based on your observations in order to judge whether your skill has had the desired effect.

- Influencing is about trust and respect, and not about manipulation.
- Effective influencing is transparent and comes with consideration for the interests of the other person involved.

I would like to wish you success – and also fun – in applying the influencing skills.

Bibliography

Bennebroek Gravenhorst, K.M and J.J. Boonstra, 'Beïnvloedingsgedrag van adviseurs in veranderingsprocessen' in: *Management en Organisatie* number 2, April/May. The authors describe nine forms of influencing based on Yukl, G. and C. Falbe,'Influence tactics and objectives in upward, downward, and lateral influence attempts', *Journal of Applied Psychology*, 76, 1990, pp. 132–140.

Cialdini, R.B., *Influence: Science and Practice.* Allyn & Bacon, 4th edition, 2000.

Clarke, J., *Office Politics, a Survival Guide*. The Industrial Society, London, 1999.

Dauwerse, T. and A. Koopman, *Beïnvloeden. Een onderzoek naar beïnvloeden, humor, communicatie en effectiviteit.* Universiteit Utrecht/Vakgroep Sociale en Organisatiepsychologie, i.c.w. Schouten & Nelissen, Utrecht, 2000.

Harrison, R.A., *The Consultant's Journey.* McGraw Hill, New York, 1995, pp. 80-83.

Kotter, J.P., *Leading Change.* Harvard Business Press, 1996.

Lyric credits

1 'Respect' (O. Redding) – Aretha Franklin, *The best of Aretha Franklin*, 2005.
2 'It's gonna work out fine' (L. Seneca) – Ike and Tina Turner, *River Deep, Mountain High*, 2001.
3 'Blowin' in the wind' (B. Dylan) – Bob Dylan, *The Best of Dylan*, 2006.
4 'Three steps to heaven' (B. and E. Cochran) – Eddie Cochran, *The Eddie Cochran Singles Album*, 1993.
5 'My way' (Anka/Revaux/Thibault/Francois) – Frank Sinatra, *The Best of Frank Sinatra*, 1997.
6 'Perfect Day' (L. Reed) – Lou Reed, *Transformer*, 1973.
7 'You are everything' (Ashford and Simpson) – Marvin Gaye and Diana Ross, *The Best of Marvin Gaye*, 2004.
8 'True colours' (C. Lauper) – Cyndi Lauper, *12 Deadly Cyns*, 1998.
9 'Revolution' (J. Lennon/P. McCartney) – The Beatles, *White Album*, 1968.
10 'Reason to believe' (T. Hardin) – Tim Hardin, *Hang on to a Dream*, 1994.
11 'Come talk to me' (P. Gabriel) – Peter Gabriel, *Secret World Live*, 1994.
12 'Ik kan het niet alleen' (Van der Lubbe/Arzbach/Broek) – De Dijk, *Het beste van De Dijk*, 1998.
13 'It's a man's man's man's world' (J. Brown/B.Newsome) – James Brown, *Classic James Brown*, 1999.
14 'Over the rainbow' (H. Arlen/E.Y. Yarburg) – taken from Rufus Wainwright, *Rufus does Judy at Carnegie Hall*, 2007.
15 'You can sleep while I drive' (M. Etheridge) – Melissa Etheridge, *Brave and Crazy*, 1989.
16 'I'm walking' (Domino/Bartholomew) – Fats Domino, *The Best of Fats*, 1999.
17 'Let it Be' (J. Lennon/P. McCartney) – The Beatles, *Let it Be*, 1970.
18 'Radar Love' (Kooyman/Hay) – Golden Earring, *The Naked Truth*, 2000.
19 'Torn between two lovers' (M. MacGregor) – Mary MacGregor, *The Best of Mary MacGregor*, 1979.
20 'Reach out, I'll be there' (Holland/Dozier/Holland) – The Four Tops, *The Ultimate Collection*, 1997.
21 'Adembenemend' (J. Bijker) – Jan Bijker, cd: *Life's Forgiving*, 2009.
22 'The End' (J. Lennon/P. McCartney) – The Beatles, *Abbey Road*, 1969.